creepy-a

Stacey Leigh Brooks

Published by

Krause Publications, a division of F+W Media, Inc.
700 East State Street • Iola, WI 54990-0001
715-445-2214 • 888-457-2873
www.krausebooks.com

To order books or other products call toll-free 1-800-258-0929
or visit us online at www.krausebooks.com or www.Shop.Collect.com

Any resemblance to dolls alive or undead is purely coincidental. No creepy dolls were harmed in the making of this book.

ISBN-13: 978-1-4402-1569-8
ISBN-10: 1-4402-1569-3

Cover Design by Rachael Wolter
Designed by Rachael Wolter
Edited by Kristine Manty

Printed in China

dedication

To all who have recognized the sinister transformation of their timid plaything in the long night shadows, and promptly pulled the covers over their head.

acknowledgments

For their invaluable contributions, unwavering bravery and supportive raised eyebrows...I humbly thank the following people: Meredith Ammons, Rod Antilla, Christopher Brooks, Terri Brooks, Robin Harrier, Angie Johnson, Brittney LaFreniere, Jodi (Brooks) LaFreniere, Scott Manty, Paula Payton, Sister Patsy Kay-Kay and Tex.

I also thank the people at Krause Publications: Paul Kennedy, designers Rachael Wolter and Heidi Zastrow, and my editor, Kris Manty, for her super powers and warped sense of humor.

A very special thank you to my mom, Eileen Brooks-Laitinen, for allowing me to tap her horde of creepy dolls (yes, they are, mom) and for being my doll Sherpa while I scoured thrift stores for creepy-ass treasure.

introduction

The insidious glint of its hard, unblinking eye haunts me to this day. My first conscious memory of the diabolical doll creep factor was, until recently, packed away in the section of my mind labeled "Stacey, age 5." When I began putting this book together, I pilfered the attic of my history for creative inspiration.

In 19-blah-blah, we lived in a small house whose only bathroom lay tucked in a corner of the basement. It had a shower stall, a toilet, and a curtain for a door. The basement also housed our play area. During the day, my sister and I would spend countless hours down there. It was safe and fun.

Night was a different story, however. A potty call in the wee hours was a foreboding dilemma. Down the steep, curving Frankenstein castle stairs, past the cast iron thumb-latch of the heavy wooden door, across a gazillion miles of darkness to the nightlight glow of the bathroom. As I sat there doing my tiny business, humming to ward off the willies, I would force myself to not look into the deep shadows of the play area across the room. But inevitably, my glance would crawl to the three-foot-high black shape looming in the far corner. And, if the curtain was pulled back just so, the nightlight would glister off

The lurking doll that haunted the author when she was five.

its unsleeping eyes...eyes that punctured the night veil with sinister menace and twinkling plastic fury as they beckoned to me, "sssStacey, let's play a game."

That creep factor has stayed with me and I firmly believe dolls are more than what they appear and have great potential to plot your doom. In fact, the dolls in this book are doing just that, and we get a frightening peek at their chilling thoughts, disturbing desires, and maniacal plans.

So turn the pages slowly and indulge in your own twisted trip into nostalgic chillmares. Perhaps you may even recognize a freakish childhood companion among this collection of creepy-ass dolls. Enjoy!

Have your own tiny terrors? Please share them with us at creepyassdolls.com.

Rosemary Hades

Teacher's Pet

"Mary had a little lamb...but I ate it."

Trudy Betelgeuse

Interests: Hiding under your bed at night.

"Yeth, they are tharp like daggerth and yeth I bite."

Wynona Kudd

8

Top 'Ho-Down Honors

Destined to be the giant daughter of a hot mom.

Hagatha Reinschmidt

Yearbook Editor in Chief, Best Spaceship-Shaped Hair

"I can see up AND down at the same time!"

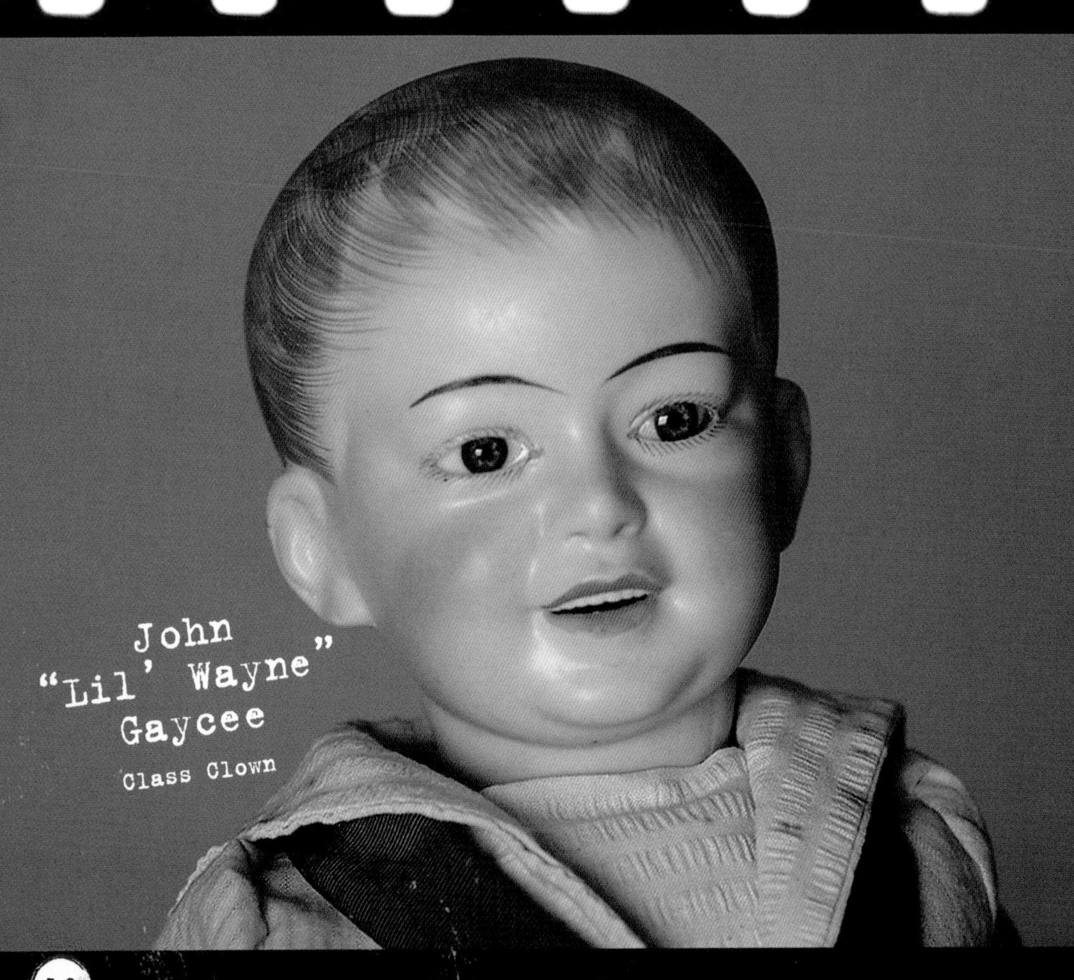
John
"Lil' Wayne"
Gaycee
Class Clown

Lizzie Borden

Most likely to bury the hatchet.

"If I was guilty, would my eyes be as big as dinner plates?"

Phil MacKracken

Most Stylish

"Don't let the sassy plaid fool you. I will swallow your soul while you sleep!"

Carrie MacKracken

Class Soul-Sucking Diva

"Ummmm, I don't know anything about your missing soul."

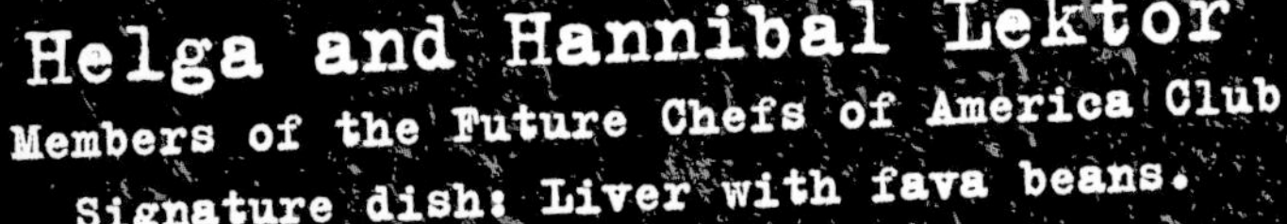

Helga and Hannibal Lektor

Members of the Future Chefs of America Club

Signature dish: Liver with fava beans.

Morgan Hairchild

Comb and Big Tease Club

"I've got big plans...big plans hiding in my big hair."

Melvin "Sass" Squatch

Young Republicans, Debate Team, Glee Club

"Aaaaarrrrggggghhhhh."

Norman Baits

Future Motel Proprietor

Hobbies: taxidermy, stabbing

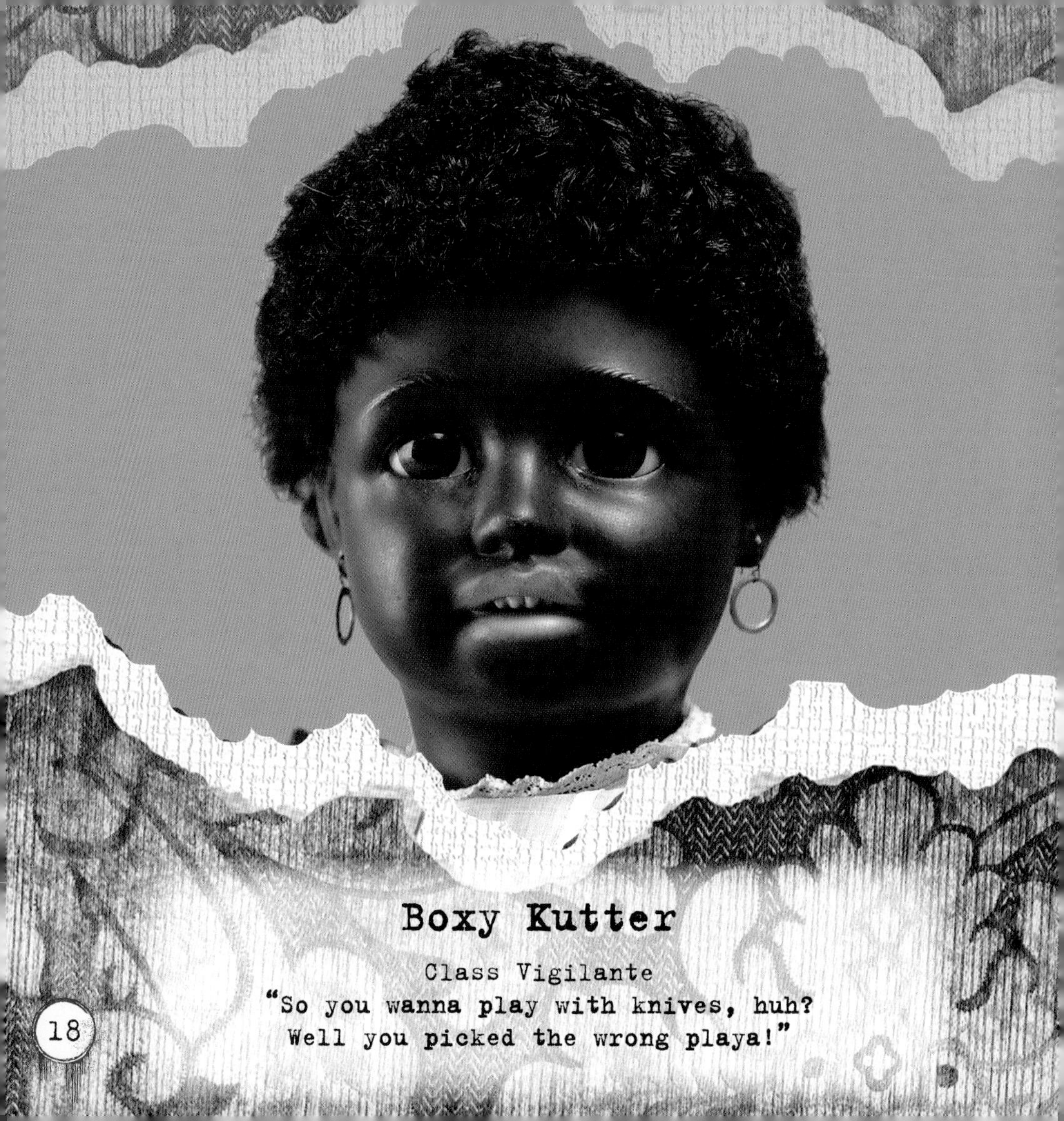

Boxy Kutter

Class Vigilante

"So you wanna play with knives, huh? Well you picked the wrong playa!"

Belva Devlin

The Host with the Most

"Don't push...there's enough finger sandwiches for everyone."

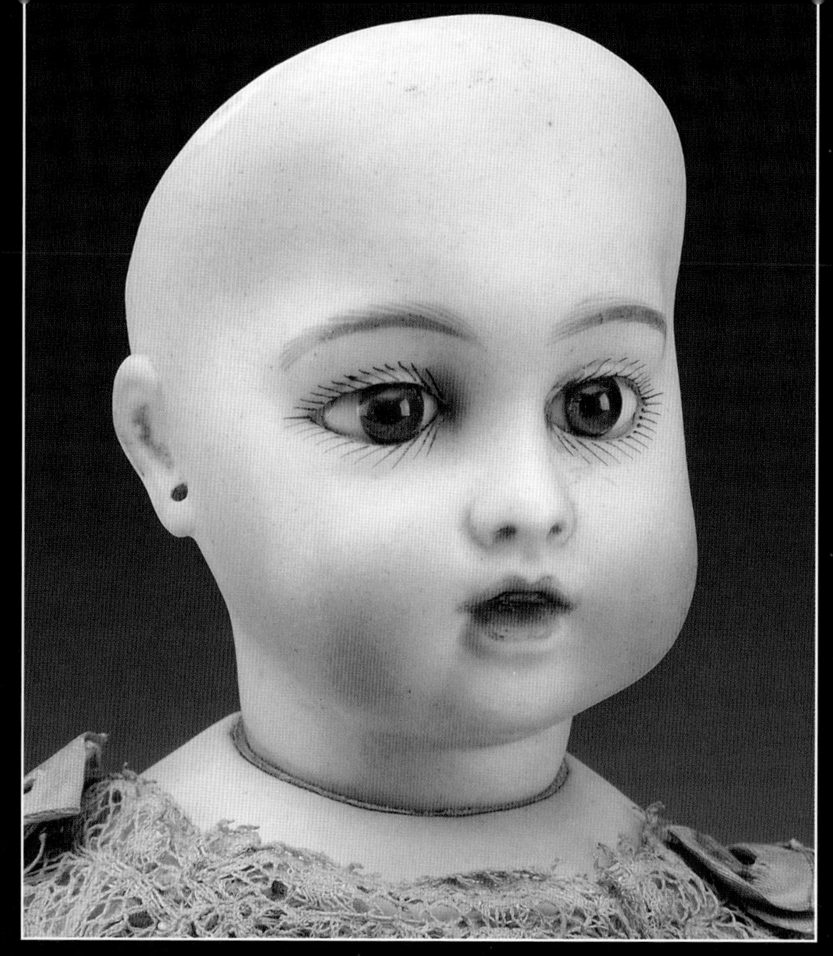

Bratnee Spars

Most likely to over medicate, over expose, and attack someone with an umbrella. "Oops. I did it again."

Vyscus and Vyvatia Ghoo

Best Couple

"Keeping it in the family."

Jack Ripper

Interests: Loose women, dissecting, dissecting loose women.

"It's what's on the inside that counts."

Allotta Zinfulnus
Class Flirt
"An evil pixie needs love too."

Barnabas Jones

Class Mastermind

Interests: crushing dreams, killing all hope, spooning.

Brunhilda Ursolovely

Full-Metal Opera Team

"Yes I know it...I can't help it."

Lester Susan Hellfyre
Class Poof
"I'm as giddy as a school goil."

Connie Fuscious

Class Geisha, Bowling Team

Rumored to have ancient Chinese secret.

Funeria Durge

Most likely to sucker people with a sob story.
"Excuse me, guv'na, arms...arms for the poor?"

Tiffany Wansitt
Head Cheerleader, Glee Club
"Yes, they're real plastic."

Embalma Baudy

Best Complexion

Most likely to end up in the Village of the Damned.

Rhoda "Bad Seed" Penmark

Class Sociopath

Most likely to drown a classmate for his penmanship medal.

Pat "Snooty" McPherson

Best Scowl

"What's that smell about?"

Sinn Amon

Young Nurses Club, BottDaFarm

Retirement Home Volunteer

"Sometimes screams smell like peppermint."

Hezekiah "Cuddlebug" Stain

"I am HE who crawls behind the rows!!!
Under this awkward night dress
is a seething pustule of dark power!"

Rumored to burp hellfire
after eating strained peas.

Bibby Jo Bolly Bob
Future Soilent Farmers Club
"OOOOeeee... you think these animal heads is somethin', you outta see my collection of human heads on popsicle sticks!"

"I likes 'em seedy and fresh."

Ichabod "Punkinhead" Crane

Headless Horseman Debate Team Water Boy

The Headless Horseman Debate Team,
with Hester "Coach" Helandamm.

Dizzee Kluulas

Political Science Club

"Umm..what?"

Rant & Chant Dance Troupe

"I dance the dance of doom...and sexy see-through shirts."

Whoopee Pye
Sweetest Monkey Lip

"I've got a pocketful of
rainbow butterflies and pretty demons."

Eva Fangoria

Lead actress in the current class production of

"Hell No, Dolly!"

"Whenever someone tells me to 'break a leg,'
I always break their right one."

Prune Tartte

Most likely to eat her own young.

"If I were a flavor of headcheese, what would it be? Hmmmm. Is pork a flavor of headcheese?"

Scary-Fate and Slashly Olsenfuries

"We are the daughters of the night and punish without mercy."

Most likely to start their own fashion empire and design clothes that eat skin.

Justin Brewster

Class Secretary

Hobbies: Collecting jars of dead flies, flying kites at night made of kittens.

Dolly Madasahatterison

Femme Fatale Majorettes

"I'm a yanky doodle dolly!
I'm a yanky make-the-noose-tighter girl!"

Phlemelda Hyde

Hobbies: Sudoku, crafting jewelry out of live spiders.

"Jeepers, creepers...
oh look!
I've got your
peepers in my hand."

FBI (Freaks, Beasts & the Insane) Club
"Muldah, you know I don't believe in ghosts...
except the one right behind you."

Delphine Nightshade

Most likely to end up working the carnival circuit in a glass box.

"I smell my future in your eyes."

Darla Dustbinski

Daydream Believer

"I'm dreaming of weddings, lace, and revenge."

Rosie O'Donutt

Most Likely to be found at Satan's dessert table.

"I'll take an éclair with sprinkles
and, oh ya, your soul."

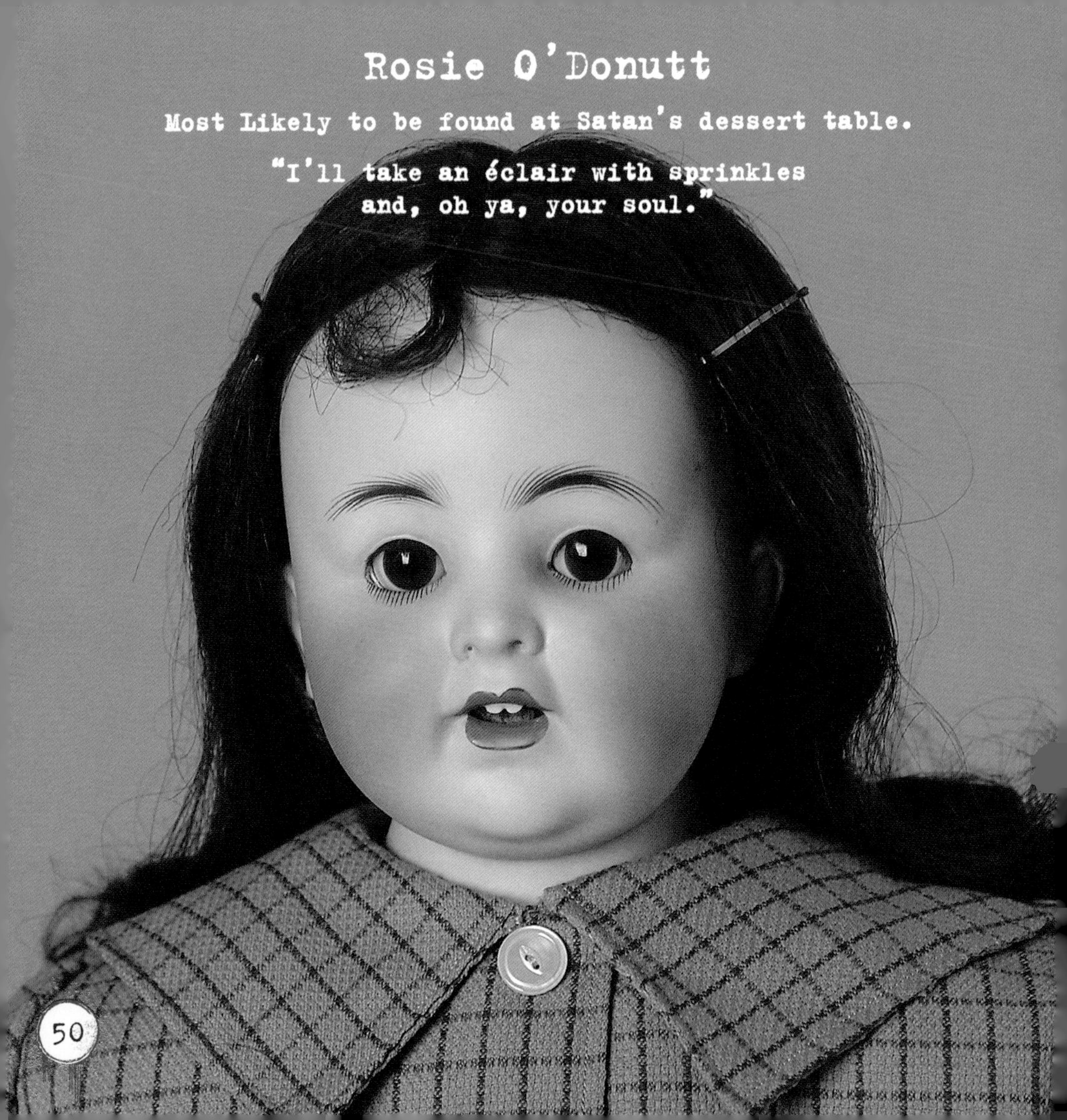

Painnochio

McSplinter's Wood Shop Chorus

"I like dead woodpeckers, whale belly rides, and bossy crickets…no strings attached."

"Typhoid" Mary Lamb

"Ewe need to want me."

Most likely to be remembered
for her epidemic generosity.

"Ooops...teehee...that came outta me.
Can I get a moist towelette over here?"

Rumored to be a 52-year-old man-baby from Queens.

Carrietta White

Prom Queen

Favorite activity: using her mind power to get fiery revenge on those who laugh at her.

Ivory Towah

St. Severe Prim Etiquette
Cheer Squad

"It's Ivory not Porcelain! Get it right, dammit! What?! Yes, I've got th-ankles! I'm the pillar of the cheer-a-mid, dumbass!"

Escretia Brown

"If ya give me two bits, I'll show ya where ta get a fresh cadaver for your 'xperiments."

Rumored to run with both Burke and Hare.

Batmortah Moon

Severe Drama Club

"HE makes me think bad thoughts..."

Orsyn "Nutcrackah" Helles

Organizer of Slay Ride 2011

"Roosseeebbbuudddd....get me a moonpie. I'd kill for a moonpie...don't make me."

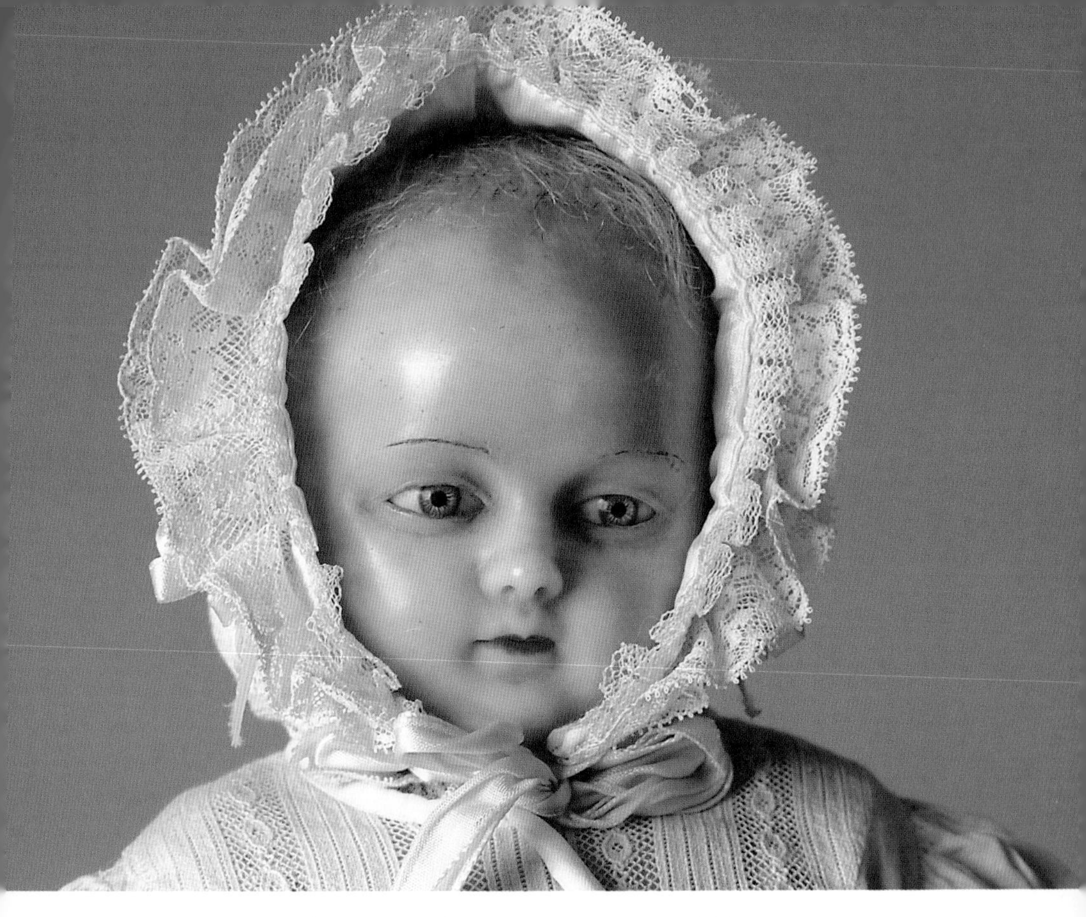

Quentin Tarantella

Audio Visual Club

"Frilly bonnets lure you into a false sense of security.
When you least expect it, I STRIKE!!
Feel my BUNTIN' of PAIN!!"

Prudy Stiffson

Iron Maiden Chastity Club

"Ironing starch directly onto the flesh prevents wrinkles and preserves one's strict moral posture."

Most Sarcastic

"*Of course* I'm not really evil.
I was just painted this way."

Velvet Drapes

Funeral Home Decorators of Tomorrow
"We put the FUN in funeral."

Inna Gudder

Swiggers Club, Dance Club

"Mother always said my mouth would freeze this way if I wrapped my lips around too many bottles of tequila."

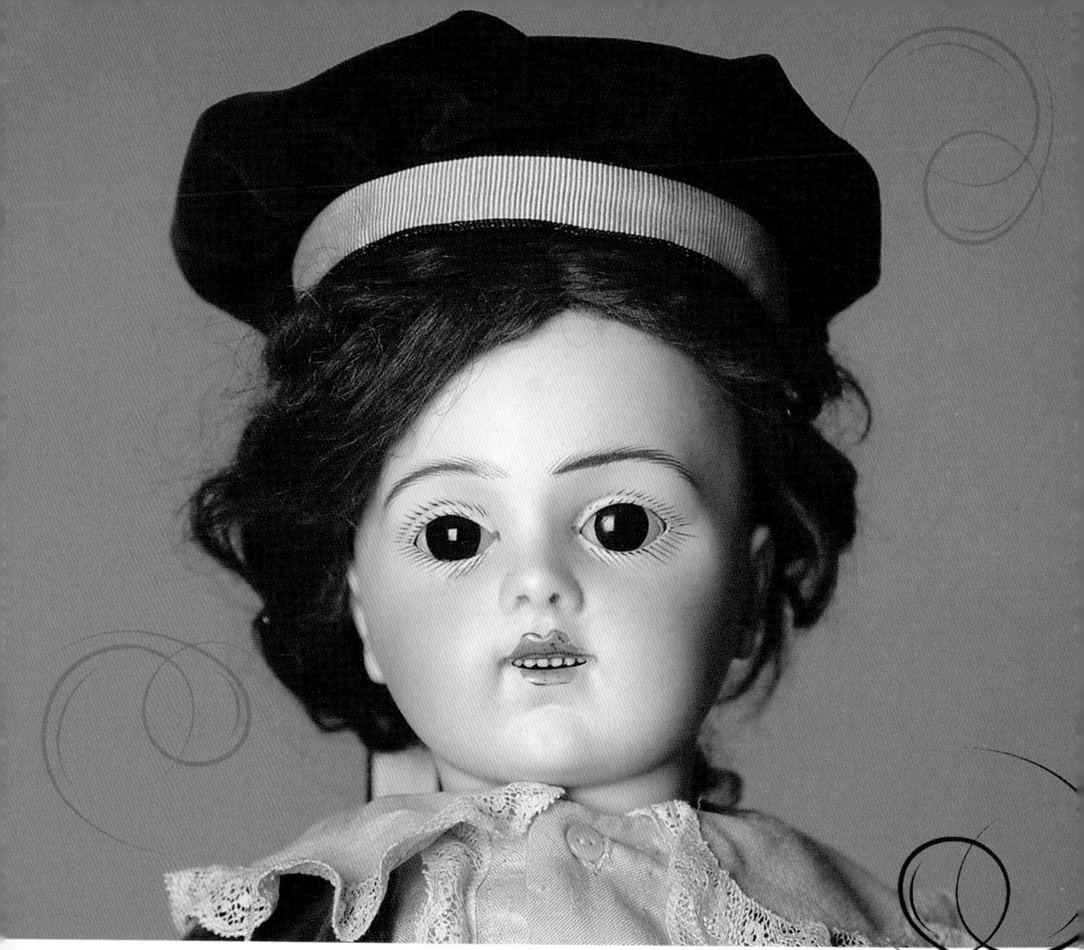

Kakob Grimm

Fairytale Literary Club, Ruffled Collar Choir

"Me loves Lunch Lady Sweeney's meat pies."

Pooter Grimm

Fairytale Literary Club, Best Manners

"Lunch Lady Sweeney's meat pies give me the toots."

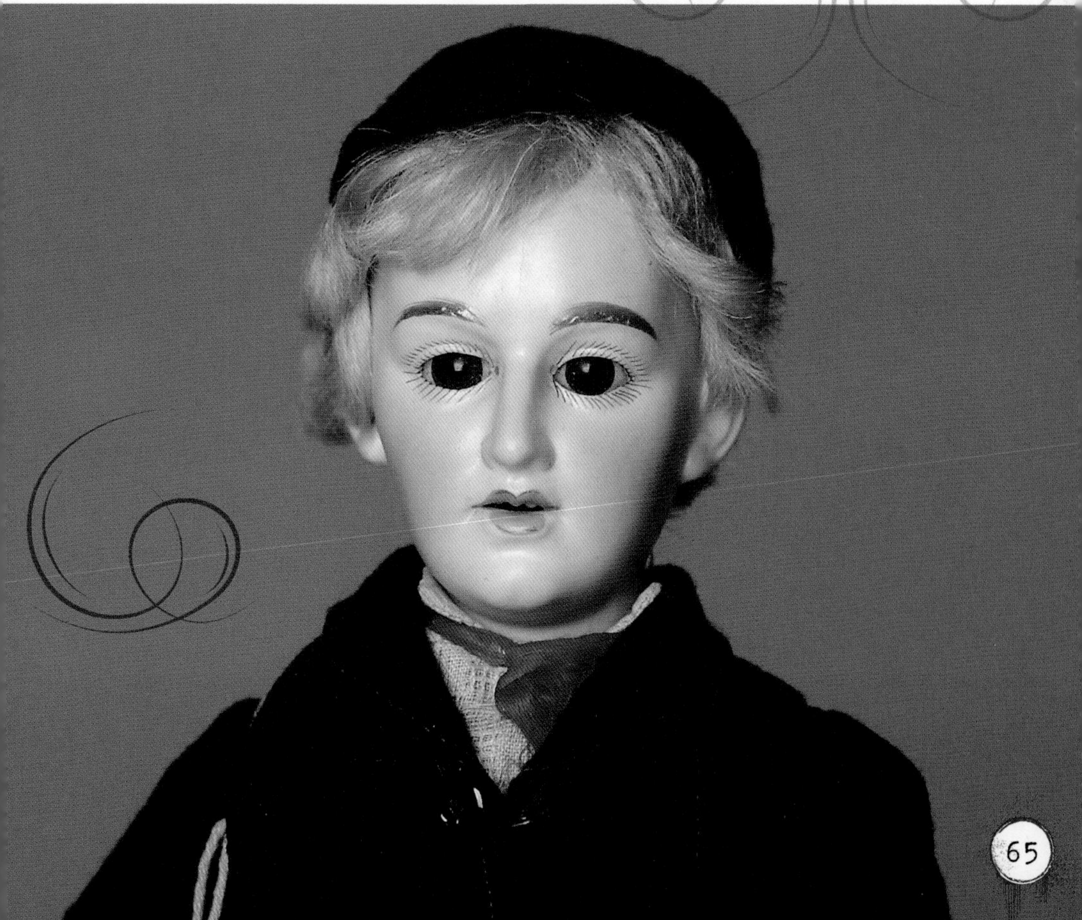

Flossy "Big Red" McMufferson

Miss Congeniality

Most likely to end up pole dancing in the Devil's Dollhouse.

"It's pronounced Stephan like chiffon."

Penmanship Medal Winner

Most likely to get beat up by bunnies.

Charlene Samhain

Class Field Trip Organizer

"Oooo you know how to whistle don't you…
just put your lips together and scream.
Of course, no one can hear you in the playroom."

Sybel Ryewolf

Frisbee Fetchers Team Captain

"Sometimes the full moon makes me do naughty things. Like devour naughty people."

Vlad Temperish

"Listen to them.
Children of the night.
What music they make...
but you still
can't dance to it."

Rumored to love
teriyaki steak on a stake.

Blanche and Jane Bloodson

Twisted Former Childstar Drama Club, The Straight-Jacket Players

"You wouldn't do these awful things to me if I wasn't wearing this ugly dress with striped slacks..."

"But ya ARE, Blanche! Ya ARE wearing that ugly dress with striped slacks."

Mestophelina Gonabedadethovus

Most Cheerful

"If there's a devil in your bonnet,
clap your hands!"

Agatha Funkenstein

Geek Squad, Weird Science Club

"I'm into human leather."

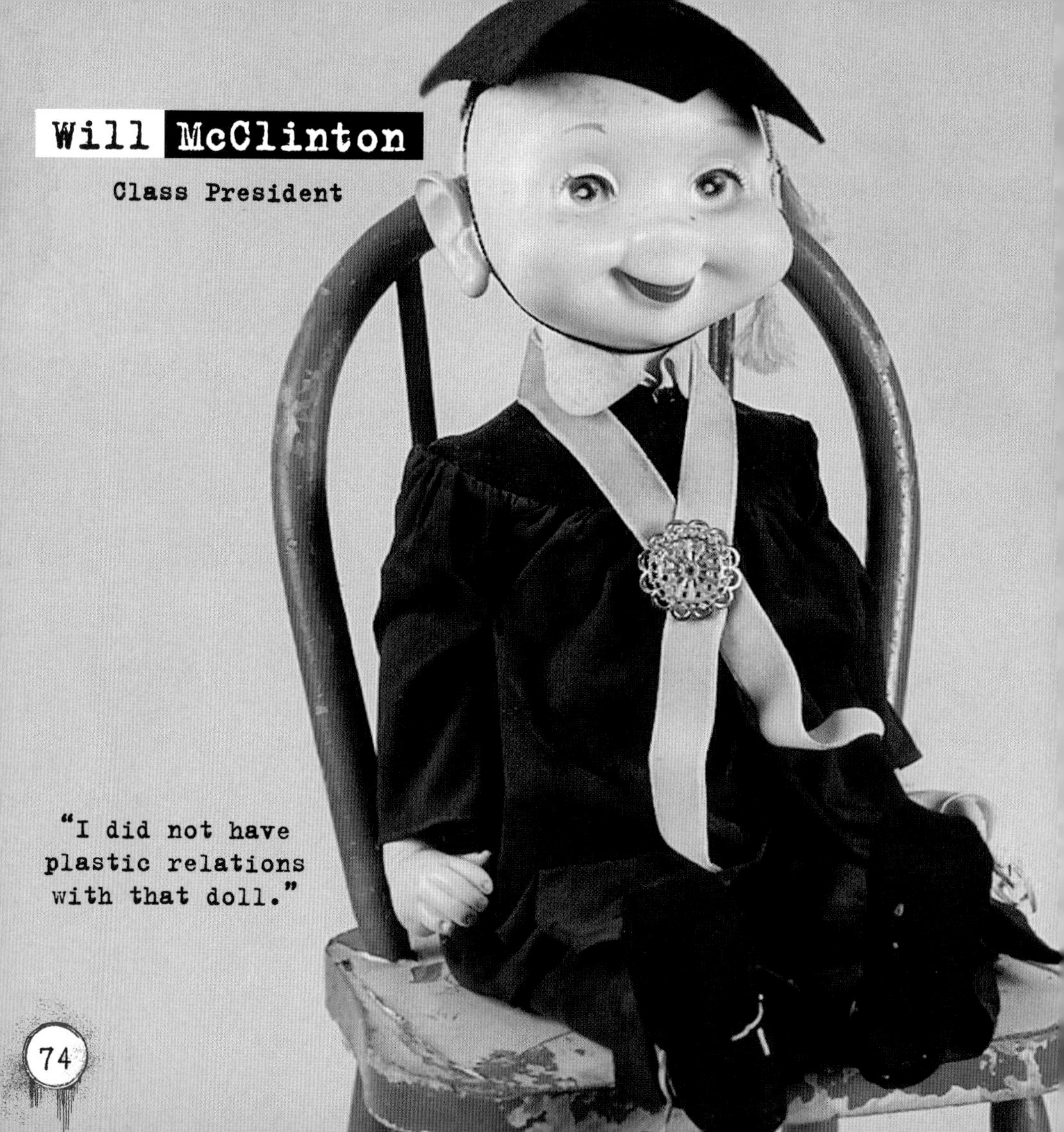
Will McClinton
Class President
"I did not have plastic relations with that doll."

Fannie Flapper

Jazz Club

"Take your peepers off my gams, buster! You slay me! Oh no, wait…other way around."

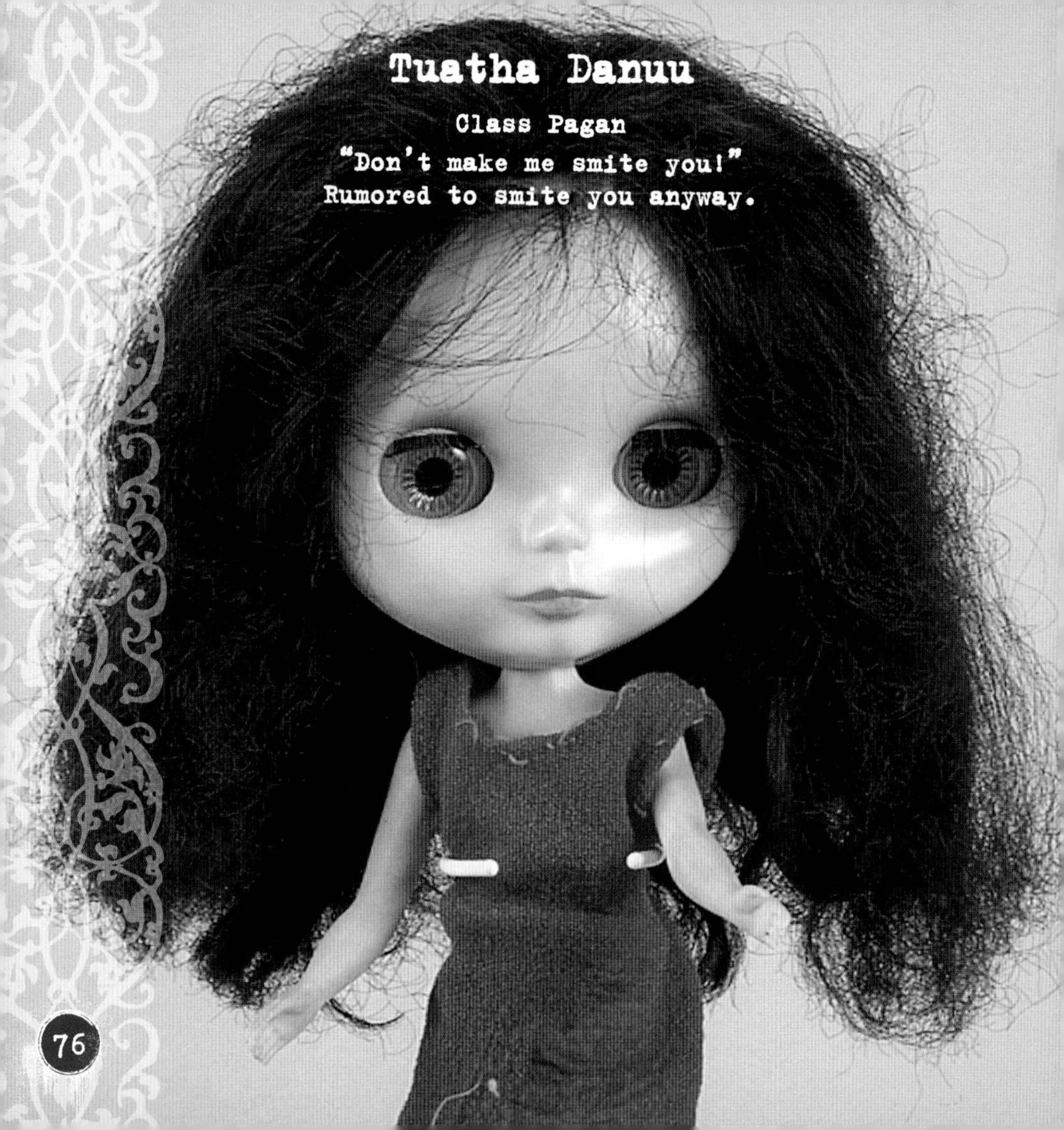
Tuatha Danuu
Class Pagan
"Don't make me smite you!"
Rumored to smite you anyway.

Veirma Whang

Nudist Club

Most likely to end up in a thrift store for 10 cents.

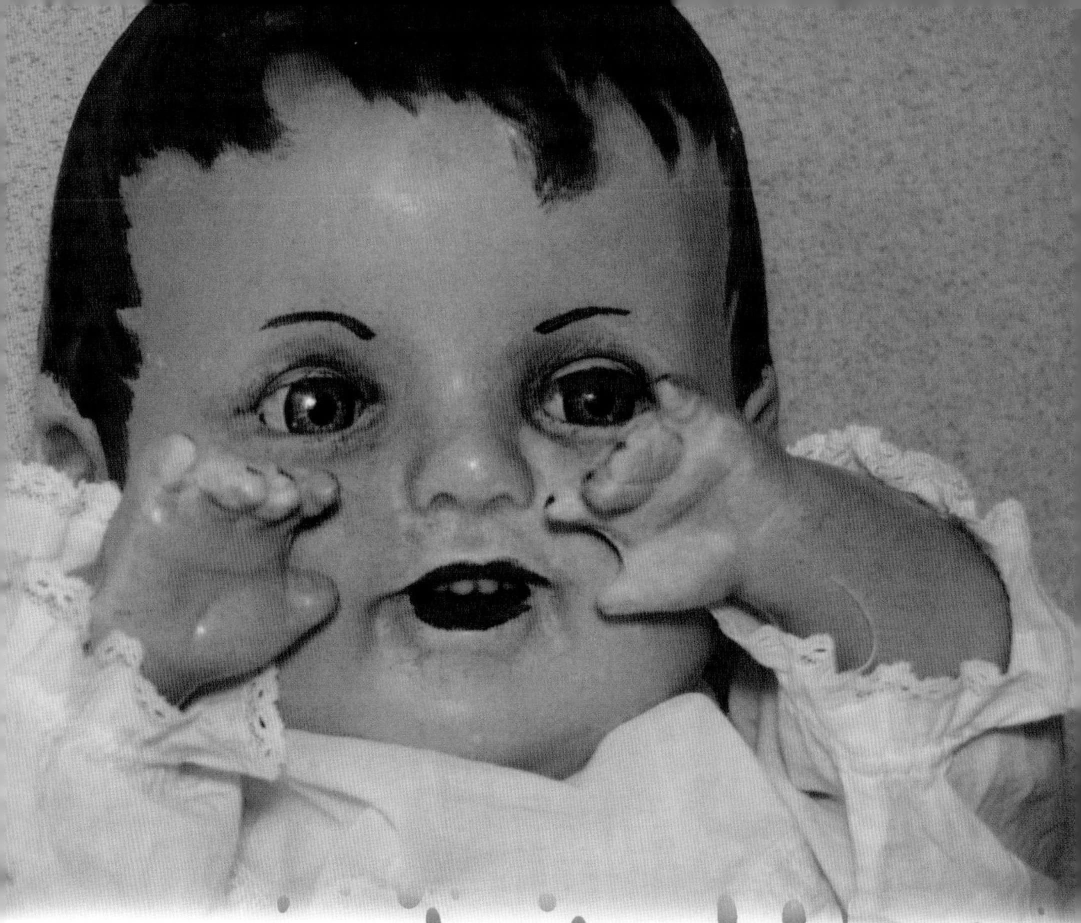

Damian O'Man

"Come here, let me have those cheeks..."
Most likely to pinch your cheeks off and eat them.

Isabella Victoria Monsoon

Most likely to become an infamous opera diva.

"AAAAAveeee Maaaassssccreeeama."

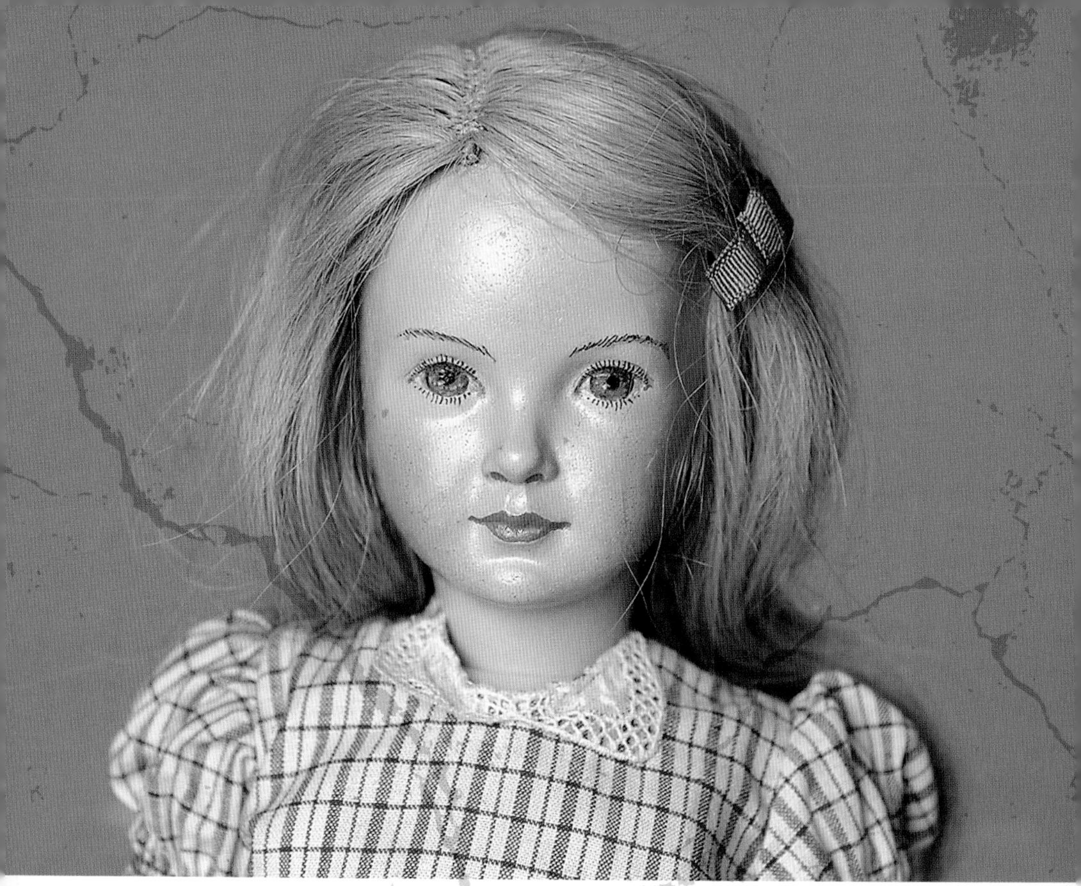

Rapunzel Tollkorn

Golden Tower Yearbook Staff, Pink Lipstick Team

"Tho he thays, 'Let down your golden hair...' and I thays... 'not until you clothe your trenchcoat!'"

Frau Hulda

"Time to milk the cows, Hulda. That's all I hear! And we don't even have cows!"

Rumored to have bendable arms AND legs.

Kevin, Devin, and Schmevin Schpitz

Loch Ness Synchronized Swim Team

"What? Well, don't look at us.
We wouldn't pee in the pool.
We pee in the drinking fountain."

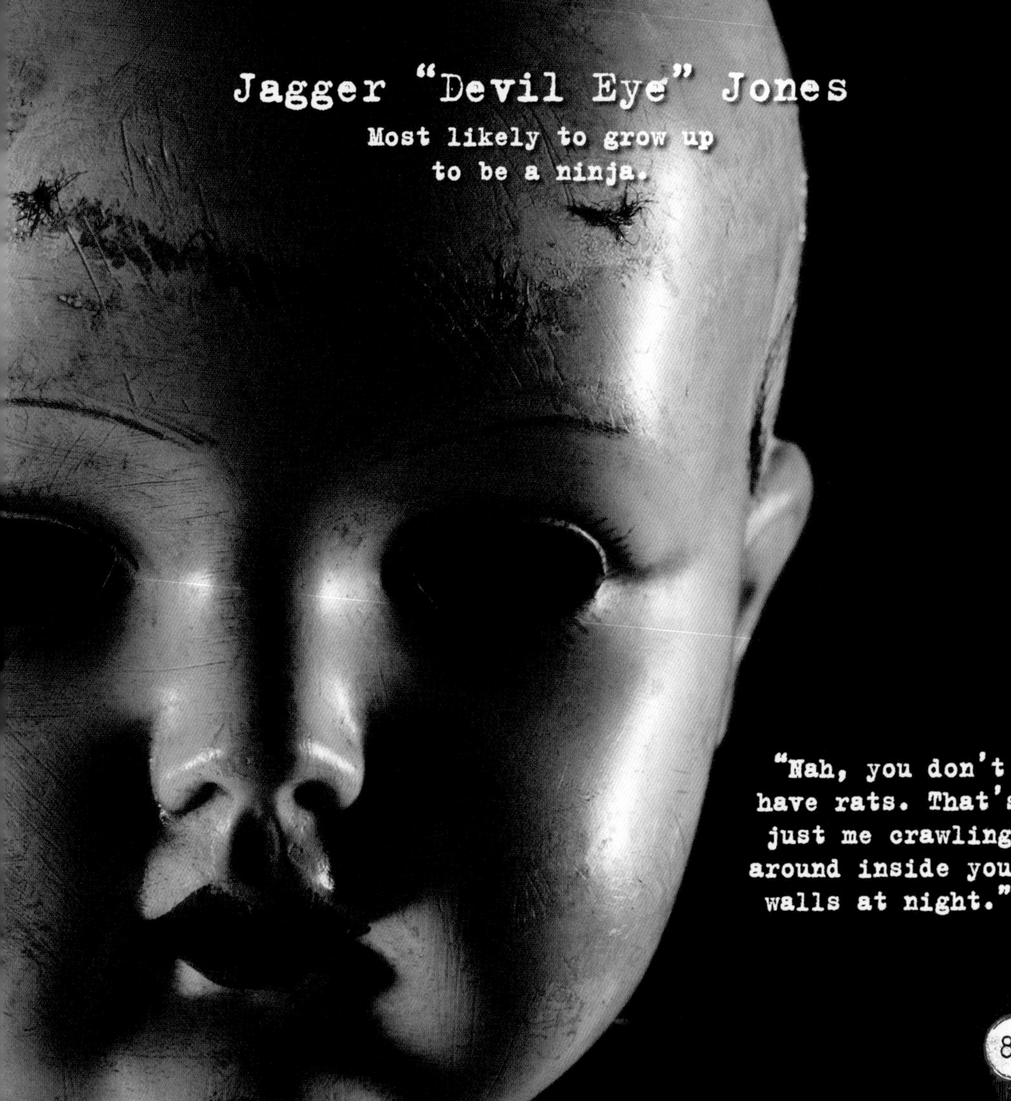

Jagger "Devil Eye" Jones

Most likely to grow up
to be a ninja.

"Nah, you don't have rats. That's just me crawling around inside your walls at night."

Mary Sylar Morgue

Beauty School Dropout

"I know it's crooked! My Flowbee was struck by lightning."

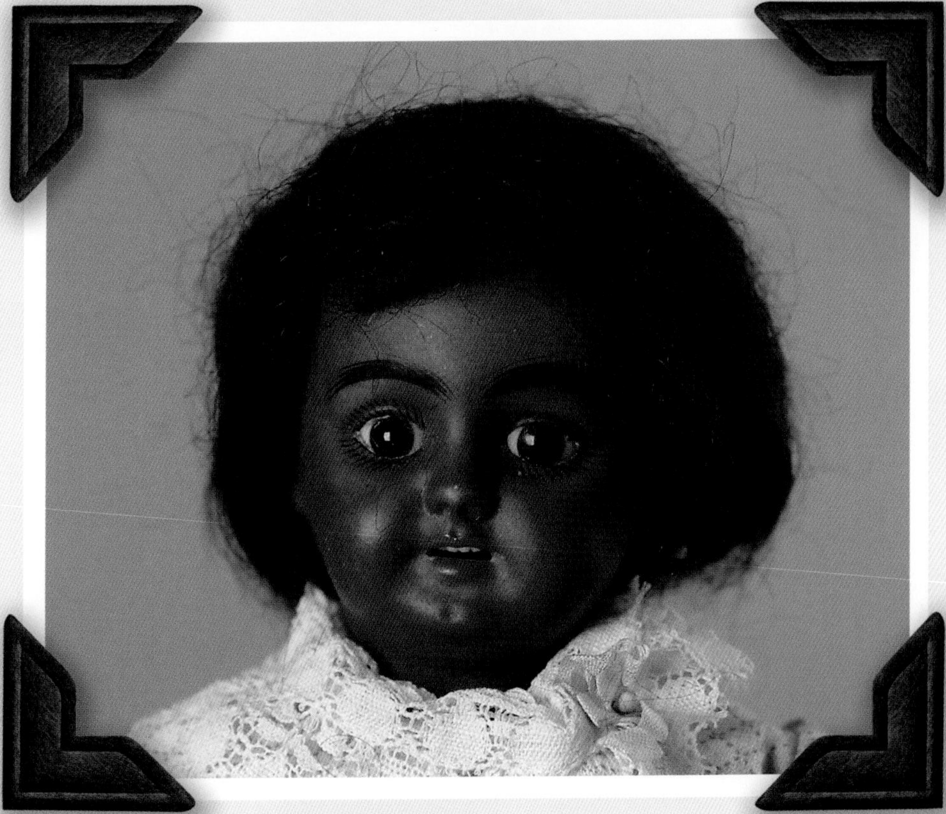

Jezibaba Yaga

Exchange student from India

"My magic carpet?! Is that code?"

Killian
"Scooter" Red
"Trust me, my
spiffy tie looks
so much better
around *your* neck."
Student Council Treasurer

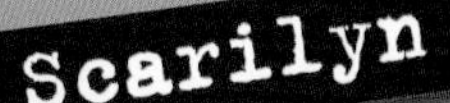

Chambers

Class Hussy

Most likely to know more men in one night than most women know in a lifetime.

Sassy Butch

"Ya, I cut my own bangs...what's your point?"

Most likely to run right at you with scissors.

Carlotta Pinata

Spanish Exchange Student

"Toro, Toro, and a little extra Toro on the side."

Scarlette O'Hairy

Southern Belle-arinas

"I've always depended on the
defenseless souls of strangers."

Kitty Hells
Clovenhoof Cloggers Club
"People in Hell want ice water—that don't mean I'm gonna give it to them."

Befana La Strega

Future Stepford Wives Society

"Nothing says lovin' like plump, juicy children in the oven. Use a roasting bag, no need to baste!"

MerCEEEE

Class "Cleaner"

Most likely to lure you in with her innocent cherub cheeks, then stick you with the plastic shiv she whittled from her own leg.

Cloretta Pynn

Most Inspiring

"I was born a grave robbers daughter. Sometimes they wouldn't be dead and they would holler..."

Little Dorothy Gallows

Most Likely to be arrested in the Poppy Field with a rabid lion, a stiff tin man, and weed-filled Scarecrow.

"Being lost in Oz is grueling. You get reeeaaallll hungry. Ya...I'm gonna miss Toto."

Buttered Baby Bean

Condiment Club

Most likely to shack up with Little Sprout in a trailer park in Nature Valley.

Annie Oakleaf

Class Charlatan

Biggest Achievement: Sitting cross-legged in yoga class without starting a fire.

Class Chimney Creeper

"Ya, well, don't let the baby blues fool ya. I'm DaNgErOuS with a capital D-N-E-O-S! What? Shuddup!"

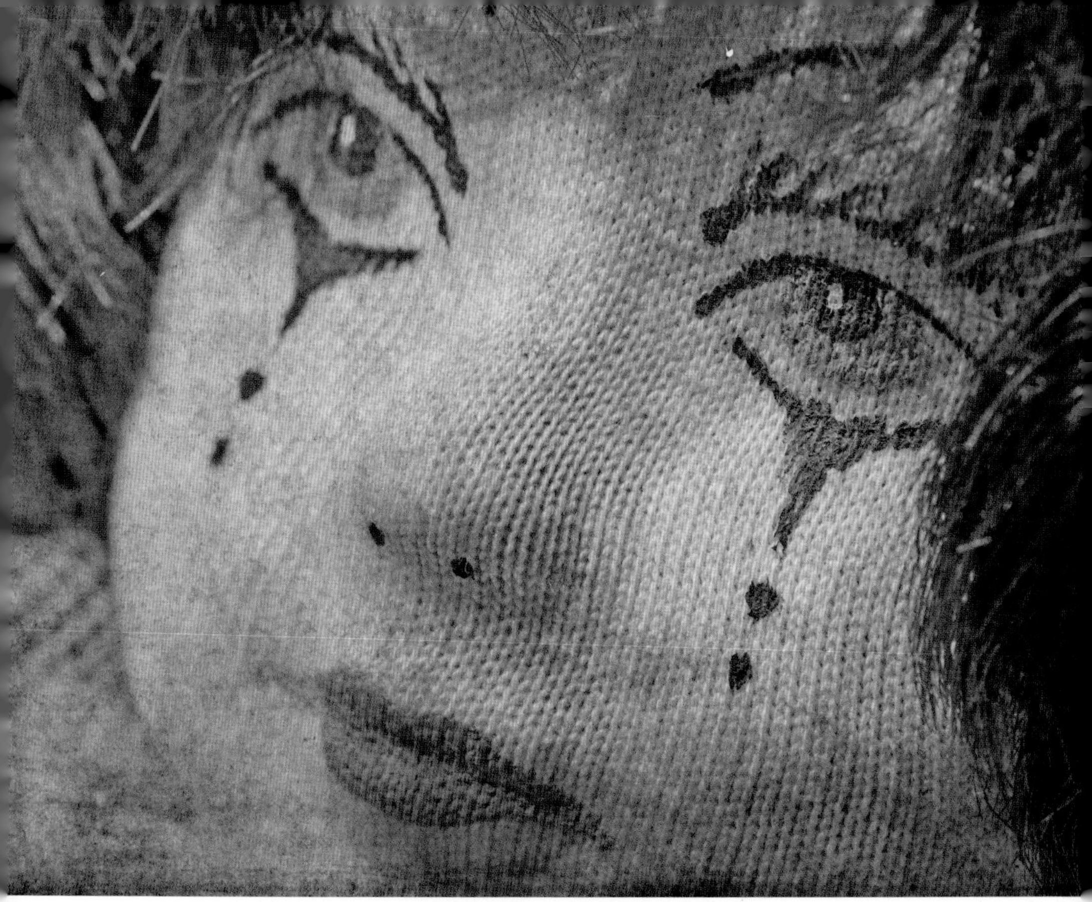

Lizard Tailor

Most likely to marry and bury several men, some of them twice.

"Big girls need big diamonds...and even bigger blades...lotsa big, pretty blades."

"Dead flesh is my canvas, and pain my muse."

Putty Kake

Co-author of the school newspaper article, "Cross-eyed: A look at myself, or at least my nose."

Black Pete

Hair Club for Dolls Spokesman

"I'm like a grizzly bahr...
all over!! Grrrrr!
It's like I'm wearing
a hair sweater!
The ladies love it!"

Dina Fontaine Flannigan

Crisis Helpline Volunteer

Most likely to kill with kindness and meat cleavers.

Euphemia
Schnottbloggin
"OMG...there's an evil
wind a-blowing."
Most likely to end up
nowhere near Oz.

Plastered Paris

Rageaholics, Tennis Team

"An itchy nose is a sign
you are going to get really mad."

Gail "Peaches" Preston

"Hurry up and take the damn picture.

I can't suck it in much longer."

Most likely to invent a girdle that will crush the Spanx empire and your internal organs.

Lexxxie Cheyenne

"Every doll knows what she wants, but a temptress knows exactly how to get it. Be a little naughty. Modesty is overrated."

Transferred to Mrs. Beasley's School for Wayward Dolls

Hellen Fletcher
Mathlete, EcoClub
"I love people,
especially
spit roasted
over an open fire.

Polly Urythane

Homely Coming Queen

"You call this ROUGE? I want MORE ROUGE!"

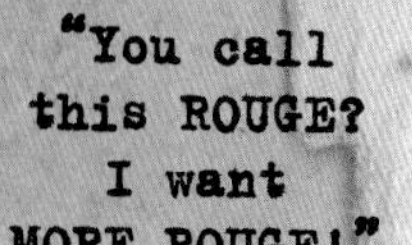

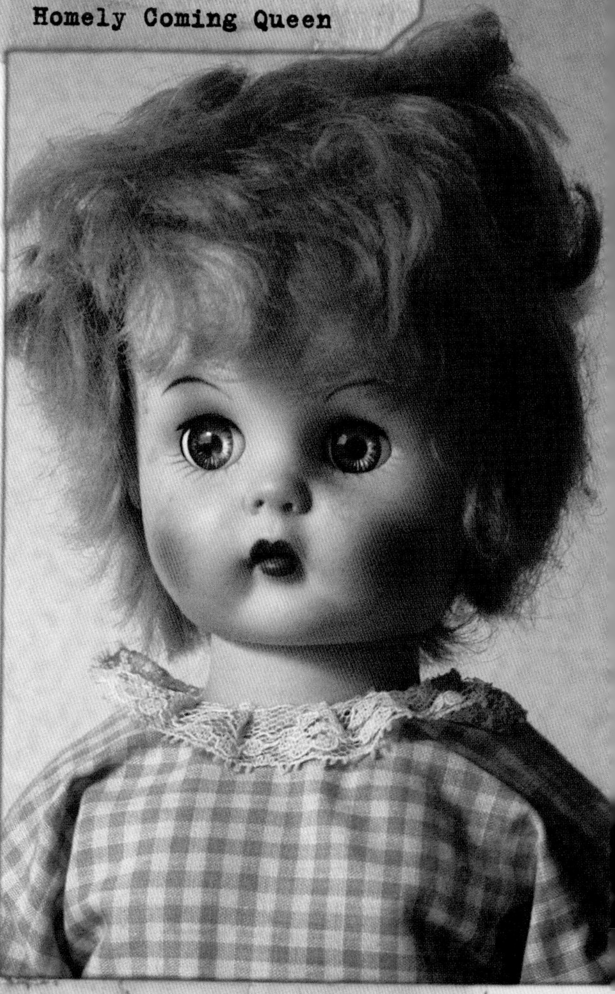

Lucy “Stinky” Pitz

Magic Mushroom Hippie Club

Prudence Krueger

Most likely to start a girl gang

"That's it...keep staring at my big bouffant. Yes... stare while I dig out my fashion switchblade..."

Elizabeth "Bloody Beth" Bathory

Blood Drive Volunteer Squad

"You're just my type."

Albert and Ebenezer Foxx

Class Apple-Shiners, Sportsman's Club

Most likely to grow up and poach obnoxious teens.

Little Nellie Tomb

"Sometimes pretty is painful.
Tell me I'm pretty. TELL ME!"

Rumored to be running out of places to hide the bodies.

Millicent Carline

Most likely to make new friends, and flesh capes out of old friends.

"I practice the 3Rs: Recycle, Reduce, and Reuse the skin of big people for utilitarian purposes."

Best Vacant Stare,
Big Knitters Club

"Knit one, purl one...
the size of my head."

Beatrix “Bebe” Gorgon

Teen Abstinence Rally Organiser

“Oh, who am I kidding?”

Annasthesia Bundygein

Class Prankster

Most likely to trick people at the mall into signing over the internal organs on the left side of their body for cheap chocolate.

"My hills are alive with the sound of screaming."

Baby Beelzebub

"Just one nibble, Mommy...just a little nibble."
Rumored to be an ankle biter...and swallower.

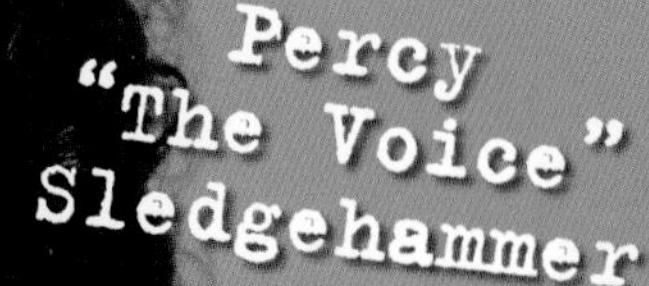

Percy "The Voice" Sledgehammer

Most Talented

"I'm silky and I'm smooth. I'm the Barry White of dolls, baby."

Exanguanatia Drysdale
Best Eyes
"Don't forget to look under the bed and in the closet...and right behind you."

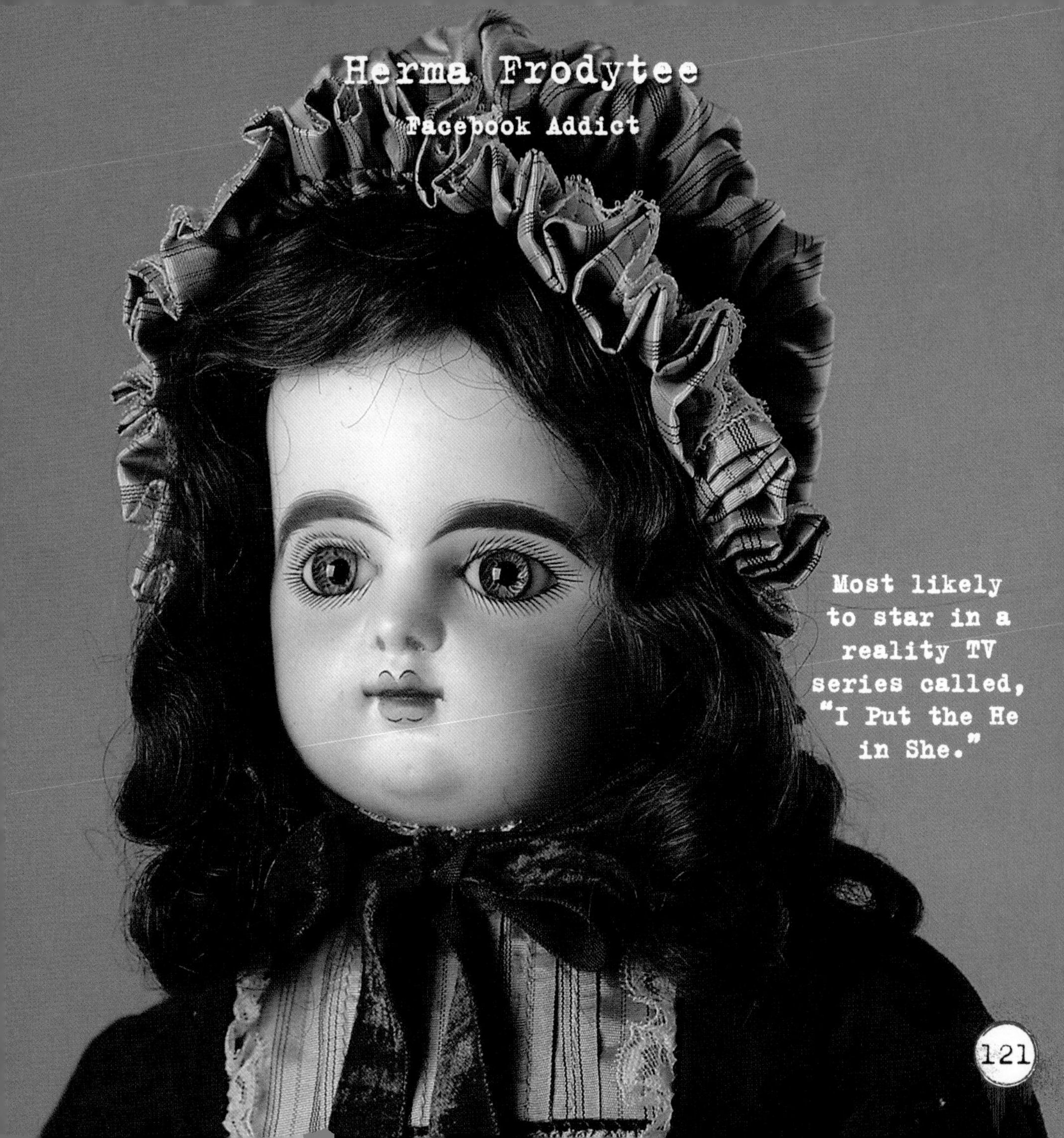
Herma Frodytee
Facebook Addict
Most likely to star in a reality TV series called, "I Put the He in She."

Christina "Mofo" Rozenblatz

Latin Club, Forked Tongue Club

Most likely to grow up to be a demon whisperer.

"Giggles" Lipshlitz

Cheer Club, Glee Club, Most Spirited

"Waaaaaaaaahhhhhh."

Sonya Plotz

Class Schemer

"I live by the ABCs of the Dollyhood: Always Be Cunning."

"I'll never grow old and I'll never die.
But I must *feed*!"

Contessa Sourfroot

Most Changeling

Hobbies: kicking puppies, stalking Tom Selleck

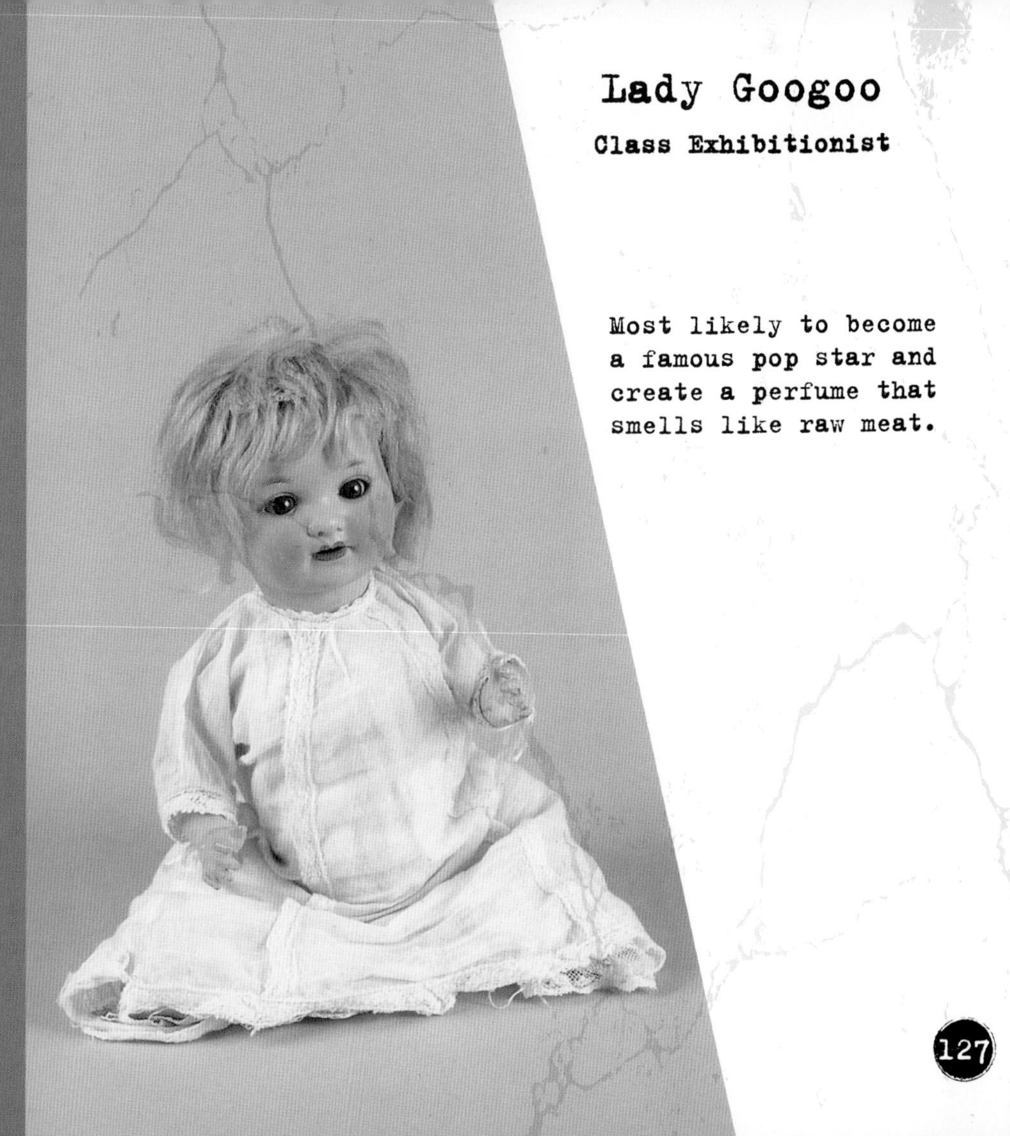

Lady Googoo

Class Exhibitionist

Most likely to become a famous pop star and create a perfume that smells like raw meat.

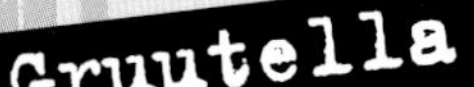

Gruutella Earwhigg

"Oh, the exorcist?

He and I had a little chit-chat and then he had to leave...through the window."

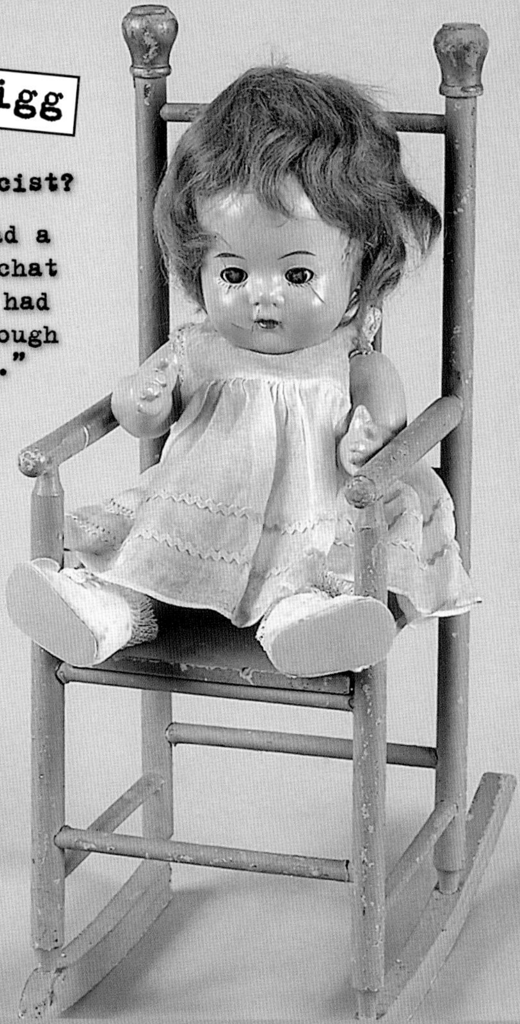

Rumored to have a number of exorcists notched in her little chair.

Yortuk and George Chevalier

French Exchange Students

"There is no other pair of French brothers who cruise and swing so successfully in tight slacks! We are...two wild and crazy dolls!"

Dottie Windsock

"What?! It was a triple dog dare!"
Destined to be rescued by the fire department because she licked a frozen pole.

Betty Rage

Class Fashionista

"What really ties an outfit together nicely is a purse full of eyeballs of people who impolitely stared at my wonky brow."

Little Lord Fart-Leroy

"Smell that? That's the smell of old money, honey!!"

Rumored to eliminate his competition for inheritance by beating them with a stick and a hoop.

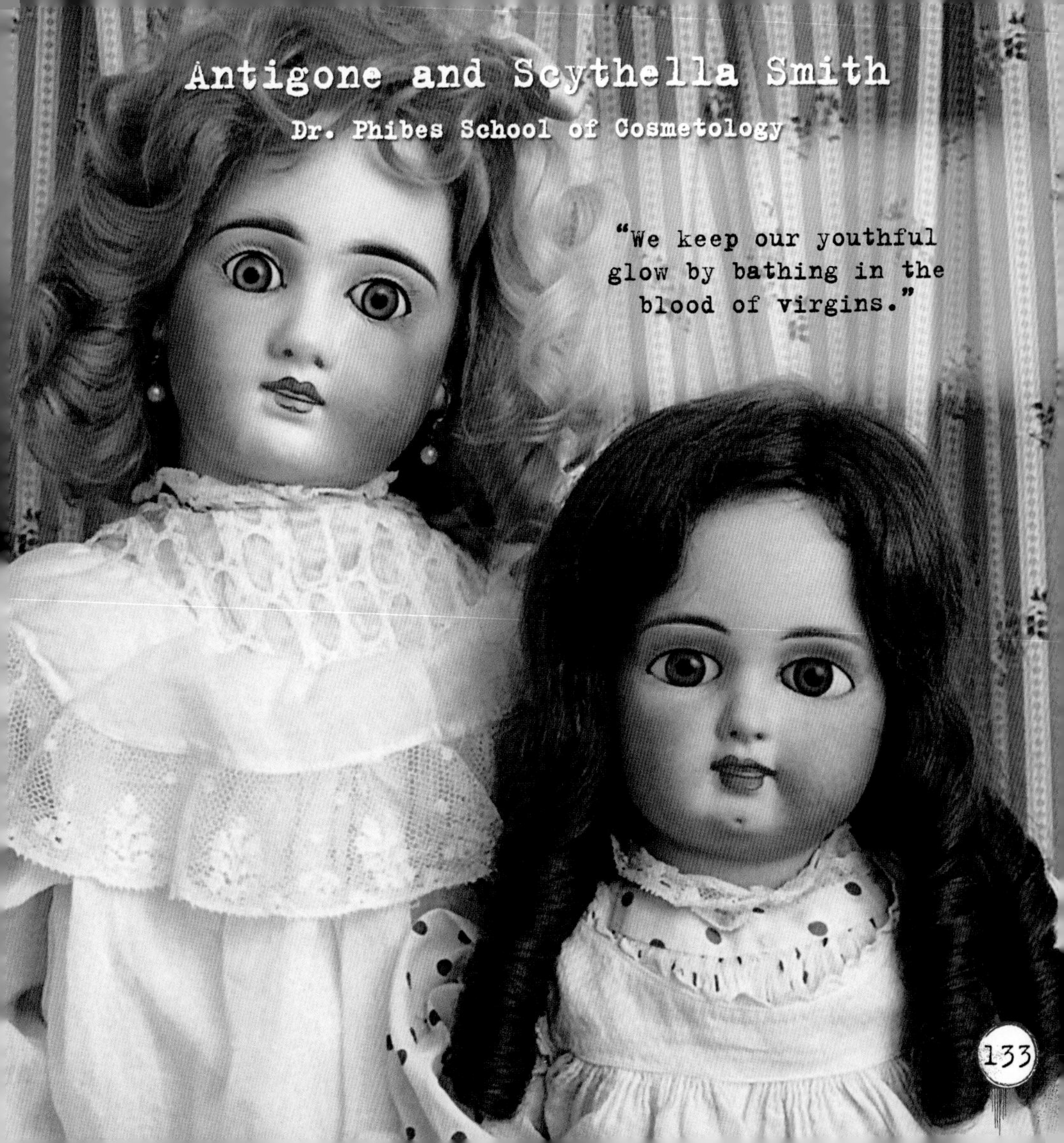
Antigone and Scythella Smith
Dr. Phibes School of Cosmetology
"We keep our youthful glow by bathing in the blood of virgins."

Melvin Humphries

Too Ghoul for School

"My mind is full of happy thoughts of ponies and Christmas. Psyche! I'm really thinking about creeping into your bedroom at night and smothering you with a pillow."

Atilla DaHun

Young Warlords & Mongers Society

"I conquer YOU...
and you...but not you.
Give me your women!"

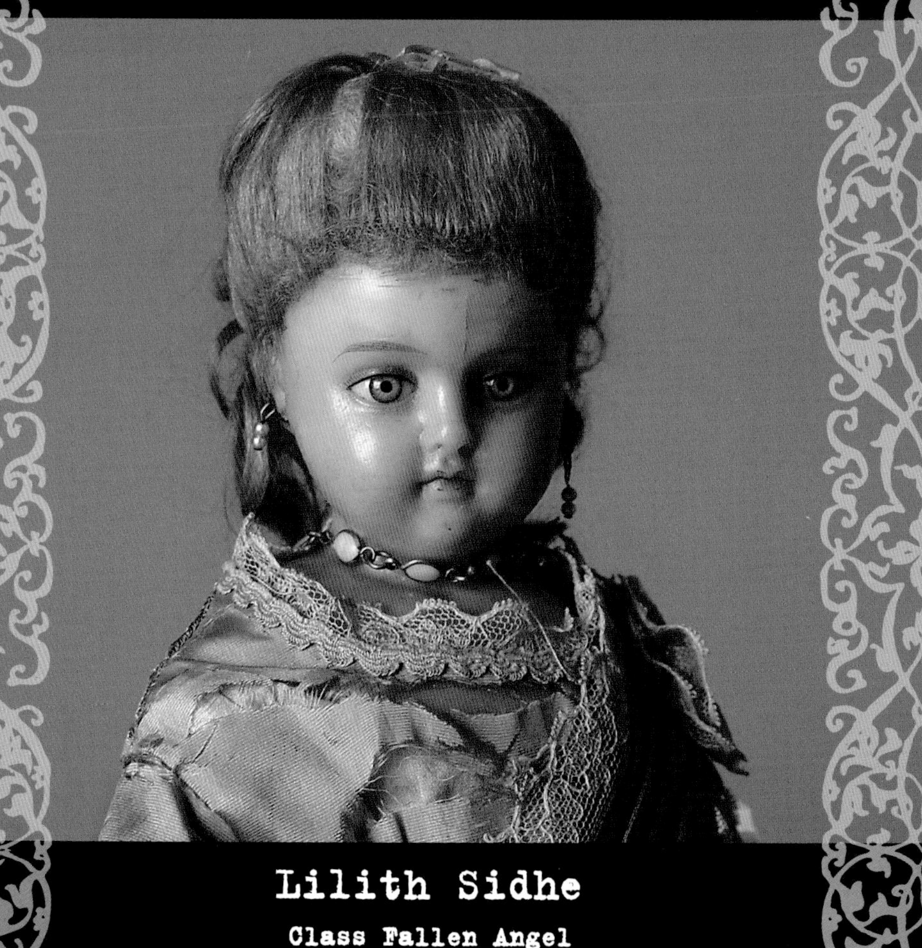

Lilith Sidhe

Class Fallen Angel

"The secret to success is maintaining a tight bun, a deep-seeded desire for unrelenting vengeance, and a pretty necklace."

Laura Inkles
Knutball Grove Goddesses Prairie-Ball Team
"What happens on the prairie,
stays on the prairie."

Maryjane Stoner
Horticulture Club
“Duuuuuuuuuuuuude.”

Vladina Empailer

Most likely to take up knitting just for the needles.

"She who laughs last, kills first."

Queenie Meenie
Hearts and Tarts Society
"Off with
everyone's head!"

Mortimer "Dead-Eyes" Charnelhouse

Mortuary Science Team

Most likely to not see it coming.

Shelby Winters

Poseiden Piranhas Swim Team Captain

"I'd rather have a bottle in front of me than a frontal lobotomy."

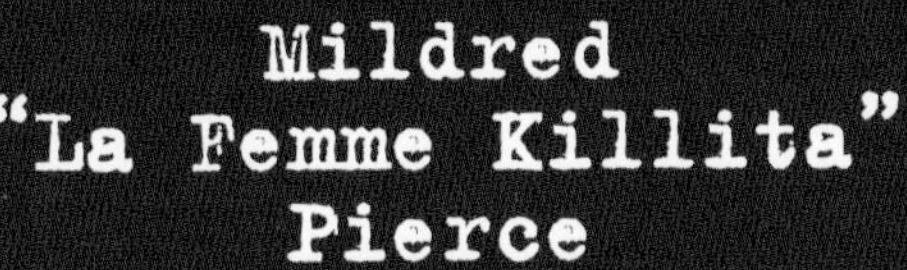

"Apathy is the glove into which evil slips its little porcelain hand."

Favorite activity: giving murder hugs.

Harmony "Cyclops" Jackson

Archery Club, Astronomy Team

"This is what happens when you run with sharp sticks. Cool, huh?"

Lil' Fester

Lightbulbs & Beakers Club

"Oooo...I smell bacon."

Dolly Dagger

Most likely to drink the blood from a jagged edge.

"I been ridin' broomsticks since I was 15.
Blowin' out all the other witches on the scene."

Magnus "Thorny" DeOcculta
& Seraphina Crowley

Class Sweethearts

"He said 'Till death do us part.'
I said, 'You had me at death.'"

Crucible Hawthorne

Teacher: Sex Ed, Government Relations

"Teaching is a crippling torment, but it's a good crippling torment." Rumored to have a scarlet letter tattooed on her naughty bits.

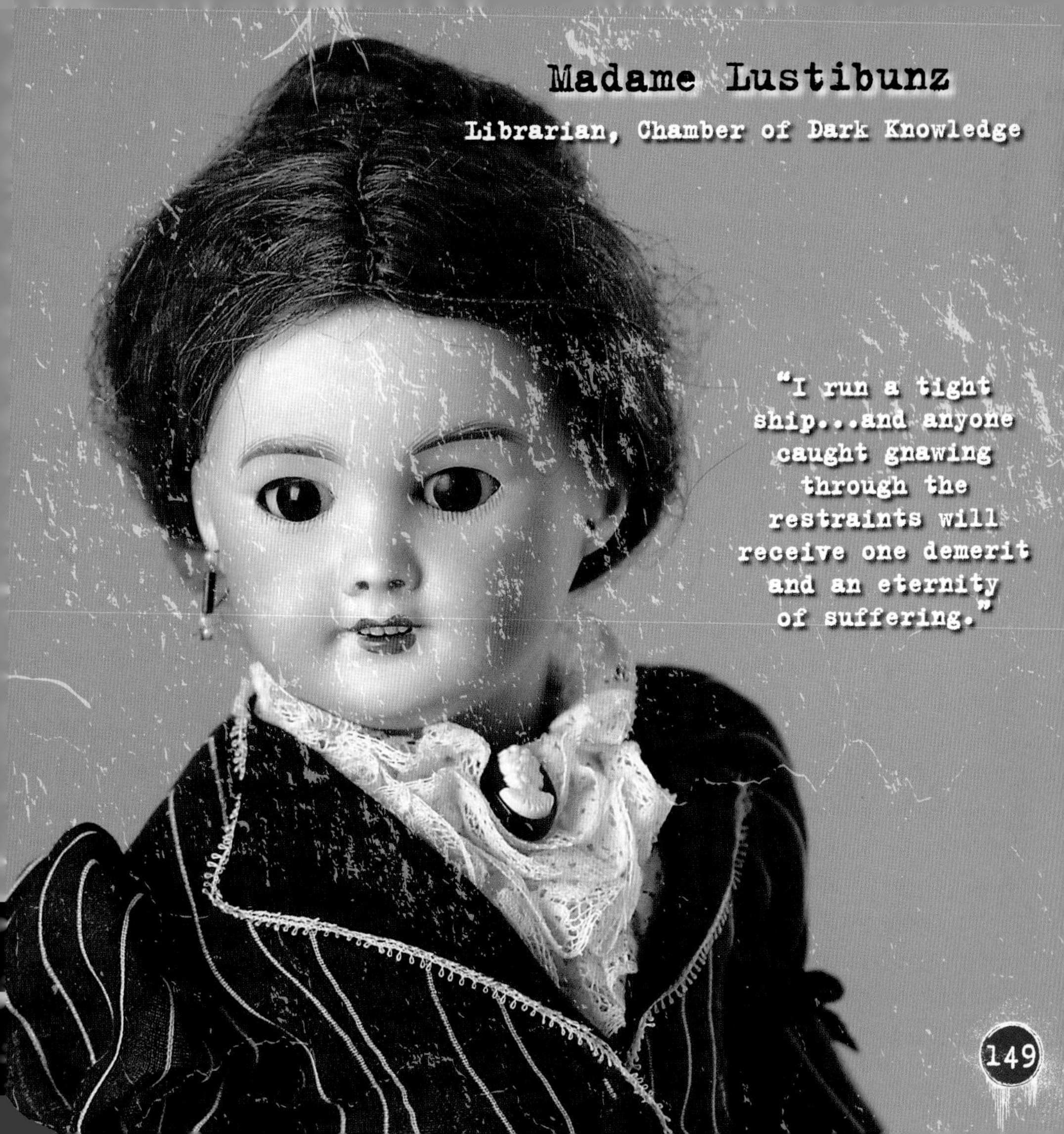
Madame Lustibunz
Librarian, Chamber of Dark Knowledge
"I run a tight ship...and anyone caught gnawing through the restraints will receive one demerit and an eternity of suffering."

Sweeney Maude

Lunch Lady

"Tis but a coincidence I served all those meat pies in the cafeteria the day after that Boy Scout troop went missing."

Libercrotchee
Mozark
Music Teacher
"I wrote you a
little lullaby...
now lay back down
in your coffins and
liiissstttteeennn..."

Madame Faustina Nox

Teacher: Advanced Abacus, Undead Family Planning

"I demand discipline, respect, punctuality, and little to no bleeding."

Miss Portense Ovdoom

Teacher: Arts & Witch Crafts

"It puts the lotion on *its* skin..and *it* eats *its* fatty grubs without complaint."

Rant & Chant Dance Club Coach

"I've got a lovely bunch of coconuts…the devil's coconuts, but they are lovely."

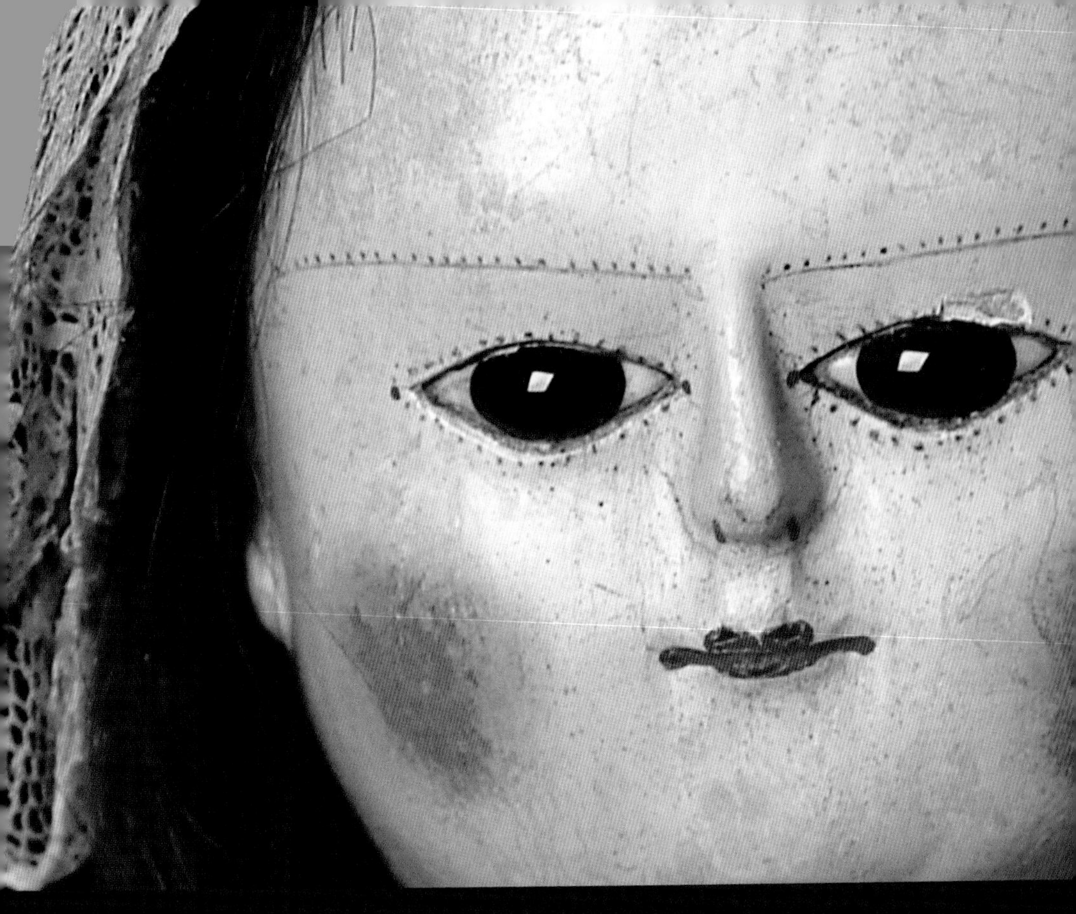

Francine Steinitz

Mad Science Teacher

"Get those pitchforks and torches away from me, you stupid villagers!"

Mr. Scaredy Doody

Teacher: Sinister Economics, Arcane Alchemy

"Two things I have learned in all my years of teaching—the economy will eventually tank and never ever put your face too close to a sizzling beaker of toxic goo."

Mr. and Mrs. Seymore Kracks

Custodian and Housekeeping Staff

Rumored to be under-the-bleachers peepers.

photo credits

The photos in this book are from *Warman's Dolls Field Guide*, copyright 2006 Krause Publications, except the following:

P. 5, 12, 13, 15, 23, 29, 35, 39, 40, 48, 49, 52, 57, 62, 66, 72, 77, 78, 79, 84, 88, 90, 91, 93, 98, 103, 108, 115, 120, 123, 130, 135, 140, 141, 142, 145, 147 - Stacey L. Brooks.

P. 137, Kris Kandler; P. 41, Elaine Davis/Shutterstock; P. 83, Jakub Krechowicz/Shutterstock; P. 99, nagib/ Shutterstock; P. 110, Lukiyanova Natalia/frenta/ Shutterstock; P. 131, Eric Gevaert/Shutterstock; P. 134, Faded Beauty/Shutterstock; P. 144, Marc Dietrich/ Shutterstock; P. 146, SunnyS/Shutterstock; P. 156, Rui Vale de Sausa/Shutterstock.

Not Creeped Out Enough Yet?

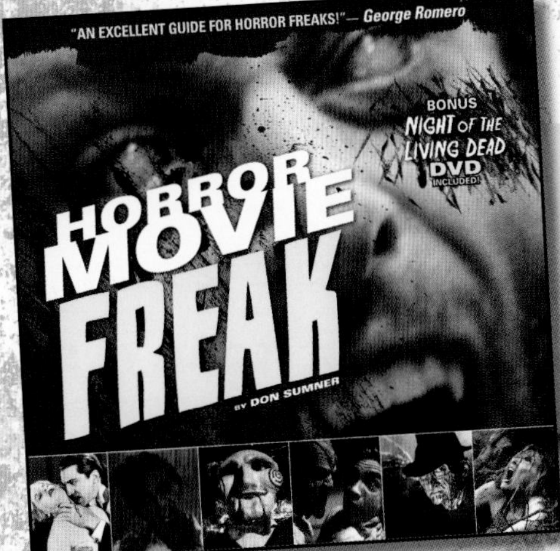

Relive some of the best horror movies of all times. From homicidal slashers and supernatural thrillers to Asian horror and zombie invasions, this gem has it all! Plus, a bonus Night of the Living Dead DVD is included to push you over the edge!

400 color photos • 256 pages
Item# Z6494 • $19.99

Item# Z8621 • $9.99

Item #Z9869 • $10.99

Item# Z8585 • $14.99

Available anywhere books are sold or online at MyDesignShop.com